The Am

Vol. XVII, No. 14

April 6, 1881

Various

Alpha Editions

This Edition Published in 2021

ISBN: 9789355118875

Design and Setting By
Alpha Editions
www.alphaedis.com
Email – info@alphaedis.com

TABLE OF CONTENTS

CORRESPONDENCE

Interesting Letter from Singapore.

The following letter from Mr. Benton, from Singapore, will be read with interest. That city is a great seaport near the Islands of Borneo and Java. Mr. Benton's search after those large bees—*Apis dorsata*—is a herculean task, and his trip thither will be well worth a place in history. Here is the letter:

> FRIEND JONES: When in Ceylon I plunged into the jungles, first in this direction and then in that, and followed out every clue that I could obtain; yet although on every side I was told there existed "a large bee," which the natives call *bambera*, it was not until just before I came away that I ascertained anything reliable regarding the habits and whereabouts of this wonderful insect, which I feel safe in saying is the long talked of *Apis dorsata* itself; though it was too late for me to get to the places where I could see this bee and still reach this steamer. As I return to Ceylon, and am likely to see *Apis dorsata* elsewhere also, I comforted myself regarding the disappointment experienced at not seeing this *bambera* before my re-embarkation.
>
> I will speak in the order of their size, of the bees found in Ceylon, giving the Cingalese names used there.
>
> *Kana Mee Meso* belongs to the *Trigonæ*, and therefore is not a true honey bee, although it gathers pollen and some honey, and lives in swarms with a queen. In a jungle a few miles from Kaltura, on the southwest coast of Ceylon, I found a small bee which contained a nest of these minute, stingless bees. A tube about ¾ of an inch in diameter and a foot long, composed of propolis and particles of wood, hung from the hole of the tree, and through this tube all the bees entered. It

seems this is a means of keeping out larger insects. The tree was cut and the nest secured. The cells are built in irregular bunches like those made by common bumble bees. Those cells containing brood were about the size of a grain of rice, while the honey and pollen cells were as large as the smaller cells made by bumble bees. The workers are somewhat less than 3/16 of an inch long, (about 5/32) have large heads, and very small abdomens, the latter seeming blunt, and abbreviated, so to speak. These bees fly swiftly, and look odd enough as they come in loaded with minute pellets of pollen, which is packed on their hind legs as with other bees. They are black.

The queen is large, her abdomen being so great as to dwarf in appearance all other parts of her body, and so disable her as far as flying and rapid movements are concerned. Of course there can be no practical value in these bees, but I tucked the nest in a box about 6 inches square and 2 deep, or rather a part of the brood and honey, and brought the swarm along. They have been fixing up their new home quite bravely.

Daudual-Meso is a small bee which I have not seen, but which I do not believe is likely to prove valuable, since it is so small. Its comb is composed of regular hexagonal wax cells, like all comb of *Apis*, but there are 81 cells to the square inch. I have in my possession a small piece.

Mee Meso are the Cingalese words signifying "honey bee," and this is the bee from which, aside from *bambera*, most of the honey and wax come.

Bambera, all accounts agree, exists plentifully in the jungles of Ceylon, but I found just before I came away, only rarely near the seashore, I failed to find it within 10 miles of the coast. I was glad to get accounts from persons who have seen these bees and their trees, and have measured the lengths of their combs; observing gentlemen, too, whose word can be relied upon. They say these bees, which I feel sure are of the species *Apis dorsata*, attach their combs to the branches of trees, usually some lofty trees of the primitive forest, and a gentleman who has often seen them, says they build combs 8 feet long. Another once measured a comb which he found to be 6 feet long. The first mentioned gentleman says he has seen 30 natives with earthen pots each receive a load from one *bambera* bee tree, and has seen a swarm of these bees nearly a half mile long. When I visited the Government Museum in order to obtain information as to whether they knew anything of these bees and where they were to be found, the natives having only succeeded in finding *deborah*, (a large hornet) with its nest, for me. I was at once taken by one of the directors to this gentleman, as the one from whom the most information could be obtained.

The Cyprian and Palestine bees I have with me are doing finely. Those left in Ceylon will serve to introduce the species *A. melifica*, and will establish in that wonderful productive Island an industry that I feel sure will thrive there and be a source of revenue to the inhabitants and the government.

Upon my return I have formed the plan of taking with me for introduction to Cyprus a lot of cocoanut palm trees, some mango and bread-fruit seeds or trees, and a species of paw-paw found in Ceylon. As the date-palm, the orange, the lemon, the fig, the banana and the pomegranate are already growing in Cyprus, I believe these new fruits will thrive and find favor. Financially, of course, it is an experiment, yet I believe it promises well; at any rate it will not cost much to try it.

Except this paw-paw, I failed to find any fruit or grain that is likely to thrive in as cold a climate as the central parts of North America. Cinnamon, coffee, tea, betel nuts, precious stones and cocoanuts and oil are, with cinchona bark, the principal exports of Ceylon. I talked with various exporters, but all had their agents in N. Y. and Canada, and desired no change. None of them would sell, of course, direct to the firm, when possessing an agent in America.

Upon my return I will see what further can be ascertained as to "out-of-the-way products." It is hard to get any prices, and would in most instances be difficult to obtain a quantity worth while to ship.

From Arabia, coffee, gums, perfumes and pearls come. At Aden I was told that the best Mocha coffee could be got for one shilling (or 24 cts.) per lb. In large quantities I think it can be got still cheaper. I should think precious stones (sapphire, jasper, &c.,) gums, coffee, cocoanut oil, cinnamon oil and pearl would pay best, perhaps also ivory and ostrich feathers. At Aden I found some large wheat, but kinds were mixed, or else the variety is not a fixed sort. This portion of the world produces little or no grain besides rice.

I have obtained seeds of a number of flowering plants and trees, some of which I know yield honey, and others that look as though they might were there bees to gather it. We expect to reach Singapore to-morrow forenoon. I will take the first steamer for Batavia, which will likely leave in a day or so.

FRANK BENTON.

For the American Bee Journal.

Cause of Bee Cholera or Dysentery.
G. M. DOOLITTLE.

I have noticed in several articles a statement quite similar to this, which is taken from Mr. James Heddon's article in the February number of the *Bee-Keepers' Instructor*: "Every bee-keeper of experience who lives in our northern latitudes has witnessed enough to know that cold or confinement, or both, do not *cause* bee cholera or dysentery." Now, I claim the title "bee-keeper" (whether of experience or not I dare not say), and live in the "northern latitudes," yet I cannot be one of the number above styled as "*every*," for I believe confinement *does cause* the so-called dysentery, and hope to so clearly show it in this article that you will so acknowledge also.

First. I once produced dysentery (I do not believe this is a disease, but merely an accumulation of the feces) in its worst form, the latter part of June, by confining a lot of bees to the hive for 10 days. A frame of brood was taken from the hive with the adhering bees, and also a frame of honey with the bees which were on that, and placed in an empty hive to form a nucleus, the bees being confined to the hive for three or four days, when the entrance was opened in the evening. Early the next morning there came on a cold storm and bad weather ensued, so the bees could not fly for six more days. On the tenth day the sun came out, and the bees from these nuclei (7 in number) were so loaded that they could scarcely fly. An examination revealed that they had eaten on an average about 2 lbs. of honey in each nucleus. Nuclei made but a few days before, which had flown 2 or 3 times before the bad weather, were not eager to fly, and showed no signs of dysentery, neither did our full colonies; nor had they eaten an undue amount of honey. The trouble here was evidently confinement, which caused the bees to worry and thereby consume an undue quantity of food, thus producing a necessity to void the excrement, or dysentery, if you please to call it so.

Again, in the fall of 1878 our bees were prepared for winter in the best possible shape, and had nothing but white honey in their hives, said honey being collected the early part of July, for we had no fall honey. Sixty colonies were put in the cellar, and 90 left on the summer stands, two-thirds of which were packed with chaff and straw. Winter set in early, and the weather was so cold that no bees could fly with safety for nearly 4½ months. At the end of 4 months some of our best colonies were dead, with the combs and hives soiled badly, while others sitting right alongside of them were in as fine condition as could be, and remained thus, coming out strong in the spring. If it was "bacteria" in the honey, why did not all die, as all had the same stores? We also placed 60 colonies from the same yard in the cellar on the 1st of November, and did not set them out till May 1st, and 55 of the 60 came out in good condition, while we only saved 15 out of the 90 outdoors—75 dying with the dysentery, so-called. If it was infection of the honey, why did not those in the cellar die also, and especially as they stood 6 month's confinement? The past winter has shown the same results, only our loss is but about 10 per cent. so far.

Now I will give my conclusion. From practical experience I have been forced to the conclusion that confinement is the cause of all wintering troubles, for surely, bees do not die from what they eat in July weather when they can fly. But confine them to the hive with July weather, and they cannot live one-third as long as in cool or cold weather. That confinement is the result whenever the mercury falls below 40° to 45° in the shade, and as surely as the mercury stays below this for 60 days in succession, bees not properly protected will suffer therefrom, and if properly protected, 120 days will more or less hurt those on the summer stands; that 180 days' confinement in a good cellar can be endured by the bees as well as 120 days in well-protected hives, or 60 days with no protection on the summer stands; that if 60 days more of confinement is added in either case, not 1 colony in 10 can survive, no matter what the food is nor the surrounding conditions. Now, we come to our last point, which is, that instead of the trouble being in the kind of honey eaten thus producing dysentery, the trouble is in the quantity eaten, and as the quantity consumed is to the number of days the bees are confined, so is their length of life shortened or extended. For instance, a fair-sized colony may consume 1½ lbs. of honey per month, and endure confinement without soiling the combs for 6 months; now, if they consume 6 times this amount in 2 months, they must fly at the end of that time or the combs will be soiled very soon thereafter. We often read, "My bees wintered well and consumed but very little honey," while the fact was that their consuming but little honey was the reason they wintered well. Thus we are able to answer the question why one colony dies, and another at the side of it does not. It is because one gets discontented and consumes large quantities of honey, while the other does not.

Now comes the rub: why does one colony get discontented within 1 month after being confined, and another does not under 3 or 4, or in case of cellar wintering, 6 months. Well, I will be candid and say I do not know; but I do not believe the cause is in the honey altogether. One thing Mr. Heddon and myself will agree on I am sure, and that is, if as soon and as often as a colony gets uneasy and goes to eating honey ravenously they could have a day to fly, all would be well, even if such a colony was obliged to fly 3 or 4 times where another did not have to but once.

To keep bees quiet the longest possible time I would recommend: 1st. A good bee cellar in a bank, covered all over with no less than 3 feet of earth, and an even temperature maintained inside at 44° to 45°; 2d. Hives so constructed that chaff could entirely surround the bees to the depth of 4 inches. To sum up, we should winter one-half of our apiary one way and one-half the other, inasmuch as our winters vary so that one winter has come out the best on summer stands, and another the best from the cellar. I will refer to this subject again in the next Weekly BEE JOURNAL.

Borodino, N. Y., March 22, 1881.

For the American Bee Journal.

Extracting Bees.—The New Industry.
H. T. COLLINS.

As the exigencies of the times have created the new industry of "extracting dead bees" from the cells, and as many of the bee-keeping fraternity may want to do so without delay in order to save time, I give my plan, as I think the one suggested by our editor, though good in the main, is apt to break the combs too much. The necessary tools are a small pair of tweezers (such as taxidermists use), a light and sharp darning needle, and last but not least, a shallow tin pan, say one inch deep and 13¾ × 17¾ inches. Every keeper of 10 or more colonies should have one or more pans—they just fill the bottom of a 10-frame Langstroth hive, and are as handy as a pocket in a shirt. Instead of the pan, a common table waiter will answer. Sitting in a good light, place the pan lengthwise across the lap, and lay the frame across the pan, but parallel with the lap. The use of the pan is to give a convenient rest to the frame, and to hold the dead bees. If you are right-handed, let the top of the frame be towards the right hand, if not, *vice versa*. Holding the tweezers in the hand, which is right (often the left one), grasp the bee and pull it out slowly and gently, and with the motion of the hand towards the top of the frame. As in the natural position, the base of the cell is horizontally the lowest, the above mentioned motion extracts the bee with the least friction. But in some combs they will stick so tight as to break off at the junction of the abdomen, and to prevent this, with the darning needle pierce the thorax as it comes to the edge of the cell, and by its help you can nearly every time drag out the too-tightly lodged bee. A cup of warm water will be convenient in removing the sticky deposit that will often adhere to the end of the tweezers. To the inexperienced, the above may seem to be a slow and tedious way of extracting bees, but a little practice will make one skillful, and if any one has a better way please communicate it promptly, as this new industry promises, from the weekly reports, to be a large and growing one.

Jacksonville, Ill.

For the American Bee Journal.

Separators for Surplus Honey

JAMES HEDDON.

For the benefit of some who do not as yet understand all my argument against the use of separators I wish to add, that I am well aware that the system of sections within frames hung in a super, is entirely impracticable without the use of separators. I know too that, as Messrs. Greiner Bros. remark, bees take more kindly to wood than to tin or glass, and there is just where the trouble comes, as they sometimes kindly attach the sides of the combs to them. Some seasons, under peculiar circumstances, the loss of honey by the use of separators might, as Greiner Bros. say, be very slight, but in many seasons they will be found to be a serious detriment to the amount of surplus obtained. But why not use a system that does not need them, and is much handier than the super system besides?

I supposed that the younger bee-keepers, who keep posted, knew that many old producers on a more extensive scale never used separators at all, and of that class who did many others are laying them aside. Bees do finish up their combs full better with separators, because as the season draws to a close they are less inclined to start another comb in one of those little compartments, and as long as there is honey coming in they finish with it to keep from *perfect* idleness. I think the unfinished combs are just so much extra. If it is "strange" that I should declare against the use of *all* separators, while still many prominent bee-keepers use them, how dare you, Messrs. G., declare against tin, compared with wood, when you know that tin is the popular material? Galileo said, "The world is round;" all others said, "It is flat," and there being more of the "flats" than Galileos, these "flats" put their greatest scientist behind the prison bars.

Before I close, I wish to call the attention of the readers of this paper to the able article of A. B. Weed, on "Queen and Supply Trade," in the BEE JOURNAL of March 23d. I think all bee-keepers, whether supply-dealers or producers strictly, if posted upon the points therein taken, will say, "Thanks to Mr. Weed."

Dowagiac, Mich., March 26, 1881.

For the American Bee Journal.

Pure Liquid Honey in Glass Jars.

CHAS. F. MUTH.

The above subject is one which has provoked considerable comment, and it appears we are not quite done with it yet. I dare say that there is not a dealer of any note in Cincinnati, by this time, who imagines that my jar honey is anything but pure honey, or who suspects any honey when it comes from my store; and I am just as positive in the statement that there is not a dealer in Cincinnati, having extracted honey from New York or Chicago in store, who does not believe it to be glucosed. There is hardly anybody in our community who suspects the purity of the honey when my label is on the jar. Jar-honey, in general, is not mistrusted any more in our city, unless the jar contains besides the liquid, also a piece of comb honey. Such is the case in Cincinnati, to all appearances, and I am willing to be corrected if wrong.

The subjoined letter from a party in New York, and my answer to them, show an interesting difference in the state of the market for extracted honey in our city and New York, the home of Mr. W. M. Hoge, Wm. Hogue or John Long. To avoid misunderstanding, I may state that Hoge, Hogue or Long, while in New York, was bottling honey for the firm of Thurber & Co. In explanation of the letters following, I may state that the editor of the *Cincinnati Grocer* had been recommending my honey to Messrs. Guernsey & Co., N. Y., who opened correspondence with me, and to me he had recommended them as perhaps the best party to introduce my honey in the New York market. The result was that I sent them 1 gross of 1 lb. jars and 1 gross of ½ lb. tumblers, at cost, on 60 days' time. The honey commenced granulating in the course of a month or more. This fact, and the general mistrust to extracted honey in New York must be taken into consideration to do the following correspondence justice:

New York, March 17, 1881.

Mr. C. F. MUTH—*Dear Sir*: Enclosed please find bill of lading for the honey sent us. We find it totally impossible to sell the goods, as parties here are afraid of glucose, etc. We waited for parties to decide about them, and they concluded not to take them. We are sorry, but such is the case. We have retained one box of each, bottles and tumblers, to pay us for the freight paid on goods here. Yours very respectfully,

GUERNSEY & CO.

To which I replied as follows:

Messrs. GUERNSEY & CO.—*Gents*: Your favor is at hand. I expect the return of my honey with all the charges deducted you feel disposed to make. I had supposed that there were some men in your city with enough sense to determine the difference between honey and glucose. My honey is *strictly pure*, and will pay you $100 if you will prove that I am wrong. Yours truly,

CHAS. F. MUTH.

Cincinnati, Ohio, March 21, 1881.

[We were shown quite recently a letter received by a prominent dealer in strictly pure honey in this city, from a correspondent in Virginia, who had ordered and received from him a keg of honey. They say: "The keg of honey came to hand on the 25th; you may imagine my chagrin on opening the package and finding the contents *solid*. In its present condition it is of no value to me." Although a dealer, we suppose this was really the first package of *strictly pure* extracted honey he had ever seen, or he would have felt pleasure, instead of chagrin, to find it granulated solid. The truth is, the public have been so much deceived with a spurious article in liquid form, that many do not know the genuine when they see it. A bee-keeper or person perfectly familiar with honey in a northern or central latitude, would require something more convincing than the mere assertion of a respectable grocer that his honey was strictly pure, if not candied or granulated in cool weather.—ED.]

For the American Bee Journal.

How to Separate Swarms.

BRAY & SEACORD.

An experience of 20 years with bees has taught me to wait upon them and not to have them wait upon me; in other words, always have your work ahead of time. Next, to have your bees in strong condition at the time of the first flow of honey. The great mistake of beginners is to aim at too large an increase, either by division or natural swarming. If the season is good, an increase of 3 from each colony is a plenty; if a medium season an increase of one from each colony is enough.

The brood chamber is the mainspring to work upon for a good yield of honey. We allow no queen to live over 3 years, and if not a prolific queen she only lives one year. We allow no brood comb to remain over 3 years in the centre of the hive; by this plan we get fine developed bees, and of longer life.

Our plan of separating swarms of 2 or more, when they come out and cluster together, may be of benefit to some. It is as follows: Make a box 3 feet long (or any size that will fit the frames of your hive), make one entrance to the box for the bees to pass in and out; make a tight cover to fit the box, with cleats on 2 sides, no end cleats; make 3 or 4 division boards; then the box is ready for hiving the bees.

Now take the box and hive the cluster of 2 or more swarms, and as soon as all the bees are in the box, put it in a shady place, and let it remain there until the next morning; then push the box cover lengthwise of the box and you will observe each queen with her colony clustered by themselves; now place the division board between each cluster, push the cover back again over the cluster and hive at pleasure.

The present season is fully 6 weeks ahead of last season; drones were in the air on the 28th of Feb. We keep our colonies in a condition so that the queen can breed up to her full capacity. The Italian queens we received from the BEE JOURNAL apiary last fall, wintered well, and we now have several nuclei started for queen-rearing, as we mean to

Italianize all of our bees by the end of the present season. The prospects were never better than now for a booming good year.

At some future time we will give our experience in wintering bees in a cold climate on 4 lbs. 2 ounces of honey per colony, before chaff packing was invented.

If a Syrian queen cross with the black drone, would not this cross produce the Italian bee? Success to the BEE JOURNAL.

Warthan, Cal. March 15, 1881.

[If the Italian bee is a hybrid, and originally produced by mating the black drone with the Syrian queen, then, of course, a like cause will again produce a like effect; but if the Italian bee is a distinct race, then no crossing of other races will produce it as a fixed type.—ED.]

For the American Bee Journal.

Raspberry as a Honey Plant.

D. D. PALMER.

The raspberry can be grown in any land that will produce a crop of corn or potatoes. It furnishes a fine quality of honey, and a delicious fruit, coming immediately after strawberries. Sandy or light soils produce a better flavored fruit but not so much nor as large as clay soils.

The ground should be spaded or ploughed deep, and raked or harrowed thoroughly so as to pulverize it. If you get plants by mail, dip them in water as soon as received and bury the roots in moist shady ground until you are ready to set them out. Plants can be sent by mail with as much certainty of arriving in good condition as if carried personally or sent by express. Handle so as to expose the roots to the sun and wind as little as possible. For garden or field culture plant 2½ or 3 feet apart in the row and the rows 6 feet apart. A convenient implement to use in setting any small plants is called a dibble, made similar to a mason's trowel, and cost me 25 cts. each. Make the holes deep enough to take in the long roots without doubling them up. Spread the roots out like a fan, fill with mellow soil and pack snugly among the roots, if the ground is dry pour in water before filling up, then fill up with dry or moist soil, leaving the surface loose and mellow. If dry weather prevails, remove the top soil and pour in plenty of water; after the water has settled replace the soil. They may be cultivated the same as corn, being careful not to cultivate too deep as some of the roots grow near the surface. Cabbage or other root plants may be planted and cultivated among them the first season. Fruit trees may be planted with them in the row.

There are several ways of training the bushes; some use stakes. This we consider an expensive practice, unless it be for garden planting, when very close planting is required and it is not wished to have a spreading bush. Our method consists in training them while they are growing. When 18 inches high pinch off with the fingers, or where a field is to be pruned we have found a pair of large scissors, with blades 5 inches long, to be an excellent thing to prune with; with them we can prune a row as fast as we can walk. You will need to prune the patch 2 or 3 times each season. In the spring, when the plants are one year old, prune or cut off all the laterals within 12 or 18 inches of the main stock before they start to grow; the second season out the dead wood and train the laterals so as to make the rows like a hedge; nip or cut off the new shoots when 3 feet high. In this way they bear larger and better fruit, are more convenient to pick, and are not blown down by the wind, as the bushes support each other.

The red varieties are increased by suckers or sprouts from the roots. They may be cultivated 2 seasons, and if needed for honey more than choice fruit, they may be allowed to occupy the ground. The black caps are increased from tips, i.e. by the ends of the vines taking root. The Doolittle, Mammoth Cluster and Home Sweet Home are especially adapted to cultivate in hedge rows, on account of their stock canes.

Farmers might load their tables with this delicious, health giving fruit the year round, by setting 25 plants of Doolittle for early, and 100 of Sweet Home for late use and canning.

New Boston, Ill.

For the American Bee Journal.

Apis Americana.

E. A. THOMAS.

There has been much discussion of late about "How to obtain the best race of bees," and I notice there is a great diversity of opinion in regard to it. I fully agree with the editor of the AMERICAN BEE JOURNAL that the coming bee will be the *Apis Americana*, a cross between our present Italians and some other race, and I believe that, although there are but few who hold that opinion now, the time is not far distant when the majority of the apiarists of America will acknowledge the superiority of the American strain of Italians.

During the past few years there has been a mania among bee-keepers for imported stock which has steadily increased up to the present time, but which I sincerely hope has now reached its height. Do not understand by this that I object to all importations for I do not, but only to those careless and almost reckless ones that, instead of improving, will cause the deterioration of our present excellent strain. So long as queen breeders in Italy know that any queens they may see fit to send to America will be accepted just because they came from Italy, just so long will some of them take advantage of such knowledge to ship to this country queens they would not be willing to use themselves, and which American bee-keepers would not accept as a gift if they knew what stock they sprang from. But only let them understand that they must send only the very best and purest that Italy can afford, or lose the American trade, and they will be more careful how they try to impose upon the credulity of American bee-keepers. There are many good reliable breeders in Italy, and those who are desirous of importing should search them out and give such their orders, and give all others a severe "letting alone." But to return to my subject. When an apiarist becomes, satisfied that he has an excellent strain of bees he should be very careful how he introduces new blood into his apiary, I care not from what source it comes whether from Italy or a home breeder, until he has thoroughly tested it and found it to be good. Many a bee-keeper after having obtained a class of bees that did credit to America and which bid fair to become worthy of the name *Apis Americana*, not content to let "well enough alone," has ruined his stock by introducing foreign blood that was as worthless as it was cheap. For the improvement of our present strain of bees I would suggest that queen breeders exchange queens from their working stock and make a careful record of the result of the cross. When they get a cross that is an improvement on their own bees let them breed from it and introduce the blood into their apiary. Thus by crossing the best blood in the country we may hope to obtain a strain of Italians that will rival those found in Italy, and which will be exported to all parts of Europe.

As regards the color of our bees, I beg to differ with those who consider it necessary to breed dark colored bees in order to obtain good honey gatherers. I have bred both dark and light colored, and I am satisfied that my present strain, which is as handsome as any one need wish for, has excelled anything I ever had or saw. If breeders will work carefully and use every means in their power to improve their bees, we may live to see Mr. Newman's prophecy come true, and the *Apis Americana* have a world-wide fame.

Coleraine, Mass.

Translated from Bienen-Zeitung by Greiner Bros.

Fertilization a Crippled Queen.

DR. DZIERZON.

In looking over a nucleus the past season, I found a young Italian queen just hatched. She was very large and beautiful, but in trying to make her flight she fell to the ground, because of her left wing being considerably shorter, and she could not rise, although she made every effort. If I had possessed a surplus queen, or even a queen-cell, I should have disposed of her; but as I had not, I left her in the hive, hoping that she might gain strength enough to enable her to make her wedding trip. Two days after I looked again and found my queen there still, and my experiments with her proved that she was as unable to fly as before. It occurred to me to shorten her long wing to produce equilibrium. She could then fly some, but dropped to the ground again. After I had trimmed her long wing down to the size of the crippled one, she succeeded in keeping herself up in the air for quite a while, although it seemed very hard work for her, and she finally reached her hive. I let her run in, then fixed an alighting-board, that she might have a chance to run from the ground up to her hive, if compelled.

On one of the following days I was in the apiary again at noon, and on looking about I noticed great excitement in one of the neighboring hives near said nucleus. When I opened the hive I found the short-winged queen in there balled, but not yet injured. Undoubtedly she came out to meet a drone, and on returning entered the wrong hive, which, when we consider her clumsiness, could not be wondered at. I picked her out of the ball, and took her back to her own hive. A few days after I found her depositing eggs, and she proved to be fertile; but whether she was fertilized on that trip, or whether she made another, is not certain.

Read before the N. E. Convention.

Best Method of Marketing Honey.

GEO. W. HOUSE.

In writing upon this subject I fully realize the difficulties of the task before me, and also the differences of opinion that exist on this interesting subject, and one that is of such vast importance to the honey producer of to-day. We are yet in the infancy of this enterprise, and time will doubtless reveal many changes and improvements where now we think we have attained perfection. Of course practical bee-keepers will employ all their energies to keep up with the times, and give their patrons the benefit of new developments as soon as they are proved to be improvements. We should ascertain what the market demands and then diligently apply ourselves to the work, in order to reap the reward.

We talk of supply and demand; of overstocking the markets and overstocking the land. But in solving the problem of "marketing," man's inventive genius is called upon to provide the necessary elements, whereby the desired results may be attained without increased expense to the consumer or decreased profit to the producer. This is a practical age and requires practical inventions, to be used in the race for the "mighty dollar."

There need be no fear of overstocking the markets. Honey is being used by many manufacturers in the liquid form, and its demand is increasing throughout the land. Honey in the comb is finding its way to the tables of thousands of families throughout all Europe, where till recently it was never seen. Thus the question of overstocking the market is nearly settled. All honor to the Messrs. Thurber and their representative in Europe for their untiring energies in this grand undertaking. There are but few of us that realize the benefits of the exertions put forth by this great firm in finding a market for our products. Their undertaking has been crowned with success, and to them we owe our sincere thanks if nothing more. The markets of the world are open to our products, and it is now our duty to see that those markets are not ruined through any fault or neglect on the part of the American producer. We must also have united action looking toward the prevention of adulterations.

We must have co-operation in marketing honey, to produce the most satisfactory results. We have seen what wonderful results have been accomplished by associate action, and by a combination of interests. The great enterprises of to-day, that are so astonishing in their magnitude, are the results of associated effort, and this is destined to revolutionize the business operations of the world. We have seen what wonderful results have been accomplished by the associated system of dairymen. What unity and action has done for dairying and other branches of industry it may also accomplish for apiculture. Association and unity of action are the great mainsprings of power and progress in the world. I am pleased to know that the bee-keepers of this country are awakening to this principle in marketing their products.

While in New York city last October I devoted one whole day investigating the honey market, and I must say that I was completely disgusted with the workings thereof. Not being personally acquainted with more than two of the firms handling honey, I had a splendid opportunity to investigate the facilities and the workings of many houses, by withholding my name and pleading ignorance. The honey of some of our leading apiarists was found in several different commission houses, and one apiarist in particular, who has probably written and said more upon this subject of "marketing honey" than any other one person, consigned his honey to more than one commission house, and the honey was not put up in a very marketable condition at that; the edges of the boxes being covered with propolis, and evidently no attempt had been made to remove it. One commission house sold this man's white honey for 12 cents, while another house was holding this same man's honey at 18 cents.

One of the four honey houses in New York informed me that they received two-thirds of all the honey sent to that market. The proprietor of another house told me that he handled most of the honey sent on commission to that city. Of course I saw their stock of honey, and truthfully say that both houses combined do not sell one-fourth the amount of honey sold by either of the other two houses.

These men misrepresented their business, and if they misrepresented to me why wouldn't they do the same to all other producers.

Then there are other commission men who receive now and then a small consignment of honey, and in almost every instance you will find that honey setting outside the door begging for a sale. After seeing all this and much more, I can say without fear of successful contradiction, that at present there are but two firms in New York that have the facilities of handling our products, H. K. & F. B. Thurber & Co., and D. W. Quinby. Undoubtedly there is not another firm in this country that can place our honey on the markets of Europe to so good an advantage as can the Messrs. Thurber, while Mr. Quinby, who has been in the business for many years and has many customers, can place honey to good advantage and satisfactory to the consignor. Both these firms are making a specialty of our products, and they are the only ones. Go to New York with your honey; see where it is destined; look over the field before you, and I will venture to say you will corroborate all I have said.

Such being the case, what are we to do? We must have unity of action. Let us concentrate what honey we put on that market by sending to these two houses. By so doing our honey will command a higher price, sell faster, and thereby insure us quicker and more satisfactory returns. What will apply to the New York market will hold good for any of our markets. We must concentrate our honey, and the quicker we do this the sooner we shall be able to sell our products for cash.

I will venture here to present another subject of great importance, and one that needs the co-operative effort of every apiarist. "Statistics of the aggregate production of both comb and extracted honey." With united action this can be accomplished. I would suggest that this association petition our national society, praying that the president thereof shall appoint reliable and willing vice-presidents in each and every State in the Union, whose duty it shall be to demand of each and every secretary of the different associations within his State to collect the correct statistics of the yield within his territory; to report to the vice-president, who in turn shall report to the secretary of the National society, and he be required to cause the same to be published in each of the bee-journals no later than the first of September.

Every bee-keeper in making up his report should be very careful not to over-estimate his yield. In the past this has worked injury to our markets, many bee-keepers making a fictitious and an exaggerated report for fear that some neighboring apiarist may lead them in the amount of honey produced. This is all wrong and I trust we shall soon see the end. Remember that honey buyers keep their eyes upon all reports regarding the amount of honey produced in the country. That from these reports they fix the price to be paid; and when we go to sell our honey we are compelled to face the reports. When we are able to furnish correct statistics, then we shall see the benefit.

Our larger markets are mostly supplied by the larger producers or specialists, while our local or smaller markets are left to the amateur or novice. To control these lesser lights will be hard work; but as long as they keep out of the larger markets they will do no great injury. They will be helping to increase the consumption. As soon as we get to a basis of buying and selling, speculators will control these small lots.

Our markets are also much injured by placing our products upon them in an unmarketable shape. Honey in the comb should be placed upon the market so as to call the attention, and tempt the consumer to purchase. To this end we should put up our comb honey in single comb sections, the combs being straight and evenly built and completely capped over. In regard to size of boxes, the demand seems to be settling down to about three sizes, viz: 4x4, 5x5 and 5x6 inches. In glazing, we should have the glass nicely cleaned and put on in good shape, being careful to first remove all propolis or wax adhering thereto. In grading and crating the apiarist should give his personal attention, that he may be positive as to details should any question arise involving this part of the work. In grading it is well to make two grades white and two grades dark honey, putting all straight and perfect combs in the first grade, while those that are stained, unevenly built combs and not quite capped over should be put in grade No. 2. In dark honey we frequently have combs that are from ¾ up white, being finished with dark honey. This should be graded black, No. 1, and all remaining combs should be classed as buckwheat. In crating, use only neat white crates holding 12 boxes, or if the boxes are small use crates weighing from 20 to 25 lbs. net. The honey must not be veneered and the crates should weigh even pounds, i. e., no halves or quarter pounds. We cannot be too particular in having our boxes and crates neatly made and placed on the market free from all dirt or stain or leakage.

In shipping, great care must be exercised. The crates should be placed in the car with the combs running with the car, not over 6 crates high, setting close together at the side and end.

Extracted honey is now classed as a staple article, therefore it is best to ship in bulk or barrels. But if designed for the retail trade it should be put up in small packages, such as small tin pails, or pint or quart glass fruit jars, something that can be used after the honey is consumed.

THE AMERICAN BEE JOURNAL

THOMAS C. NEWMAN.
Editor and Proprietor.
CHICAGO, ILL., APRIL 6, 1881.

The Lessons of the Hour.

"Sweet are the uses of adversity," is a trite remark credited to Shakespeare, we believe. The winter of 1880-1 will long be known as one of the most severe in its nature and direful in its effects, not only in America but throughout the world.

A gentleman from Minnesota assures us that in the southern part of that State fully 10 feet of snow has fallen since the great storm of Oct. 14. Losses and privations have been *the rule* during the past 5 or 6 months. Fuel has been so scarce that in some places even the "liberty pole" has been sacrificed for use as fuel; those sections cut off from communication have been deprived of tea, coffee and sugar, and the coffee-mill has been made to serve the purpose of the flour-mill, to grind wheat for family use.

Heavy sleet storms have destroyed the timber, the principal sufferers being peach, soft maple, hickory and elm trees.

Birds, sheep, cattle and hogs have perished by thousands, being deprived of food and shelter and cut off from succor by the waves of death from the north and west, and the oft-repeated blizzard. Even mankind is no exception—untold numbers have been sacrificed upon the altar of the storm-king. Snow, hail, wind, blinding storm and blizzard-blast have united with poisoned air and miasmatic vapor to sweep men, women and children into the tomb, and is it any wonder that our pets—the bees—should suffer in common with all other forms of life?

But how difficult it is to discover the "sweet uses" of all this adversity! True, it may point out the more hardy kinds of trees, insects, birds and stock, to withstand the rigors of such seasons—upon the principle of "the survival of the fittest"—and it may teach men a valuable lesson on the necessity of securing more perfect ventilation, drainage and pure water.

When the unprecedented season shall have passed, let us try to fathom these deep lessons in respect to our bees. Perhaps there is a lesson to be learned here which we could learn in no other way. Close observation and profound study will no doubt be amply rewarded. "Let patience have her perfect work."

☞ Dr. Ehrick Parmly, the genial Recording Secretary of the North American Bee-Keepers' Society, made us a very pleasant call last Thursday afternoon, on his return from a three weeks' tour through Colorado. We are glad to say the Doctor was looking and feeling remarkably well after his extended trip, and his jovial good nature done much to banish the gloom occasioned by the drizzling and monotonous snow which was then falling.

Is Bee-Keeping a Failure?

Now that the winter is drawing to a close, and the chilling blasts are becoming more fitful and spasmodic under the tardy but certain approach of spring, we begin to contemplate with an inward feeling of gratification the genial sunshine and gentle showers with which Nature will awaken to life; the far-stretching fields clothed in emerald green, the lawns and lanes with their grassy carpets, the air laden with the sweet perfume of the blossoms in garden and orchard, the trees in forest and grove animated with the feathered songsters whose little lives seem an incarnation of happy melody—all these will combine to help us forget the dreary hours of the past, and with keener zest enjoy the future. But how many will miss the cheerful hum of the myriads of toiling bees, whose flitting wings were wont to bear them from flower to flower, where they gathered nectar fit for a banquet of the gods.

We can scarcely wonder that many have become discouraged and almost doubt whether bee-keeping pays, when they think of the meager honey yields of two successive summers, and view the untenanted hives and soiled combs which are left as the sequel to their cherished hopes for the future. However, none should be too hasty in passing judgment. With the hives and combs already provided, more than one-half the original investment is saved, and with a propitious season for the present, our losses will be made good with a credit in our favor on the balance sheet. We cannot expect bee-keeping to be profitable every season, any more than any other special branch of industry which is dependent upon natural causes, but we can with forethought, industry and systematic perseverance, make it as reliable as any other, and now that many will be compelled to begin anew (or comparatively so), we suggest that they begin aright. It will not be a guaranty of success that they use the best hive, nor that they have an abundance of bees; a familiarity with all the recognized authorities and a mind crammed with theories, will often fail; the industrious brown bee will seek in vain, the gold-banded Italian bee will tire in its flight, and even *Apis dorsata* will view its stores with dismay, if there be no nectar-laden bloom from which to gather.

Now is the time to invest for the future. Every dollar judiciously paid out for seeds of honey plants will bear compound interest—will be "bread cast upon the waters." The traditional two or three weeks of honey-flow can, with a trifling expenditure, be made to last more than as many months; a succession of bloom can be secured, so that should northerly winds or wet weather prevail for a time, it would not carry dismay to our hopes and starvation to our bees. If, as we hope and confidently believe, the present should prove an unparalleled honey season, it will ameliorate the only tenable objection to melilot or sweet clover, which is that it blooms but little or none the first season; and we can well wait till another season for our "sweet" reward from it. There are many other plants which we believe would repay cultivation in honey alone, but not one that will bear comparison with this Esau of the vegetable kingdom. Never was a better time to start in right than now, and never can we truthfully say bee-keeping is more hazardous than other industries, or less remunerative, until we have made some provision against natural failures and seasonable disasters. Every bee-keeper should, in justice to himself, test this matter of planting on a sufficiently extensive scale to satisfy himself. We feel confident of the verdict.

Law Against Adulteration in N. Y.

We have received the following copy of the bill against adulteration, referred to on page 92 of the BEE JOURNAL for March 23. Mr. L. C.

Root remarks: "The readers of the BEE JOURNAL are, no doubt, interested in the progress being made regarding the bill upon which action was taken at the late session of the Northeastern Bee-keeper's Association. The subject is one of marked interest to bee-keepers in general. I send you a copy of the bill, which may be of interest and which shows the progress thus far made."

> ASSEMBLY OF NEW YORK.—Introduced by Mr. Root—read twice and referred to the committee on trade and manufactures—reported favorably from said committee and committed to the committee of the whole.
>
> AN ACT, To prevent fraud in the adulteration of sugars, syrups, molasses and honey.

The people of the State of New York, represented in Senate and Assembly, do enact as follows:

SEC. 1. Any person, company or corporation engaged in the manufacture, refining or mixing of sugars, syrups, molasses or honey for sale, who shall mix the same with glucose or grape sugar or any other article of adulteration, shall, before selling or offering the same for sale, cause to be marked on the cask or package in which it is contained, the percentage of glucose or adulteration therein contained, such mark or label shall be in plain Roman capital letters, not less than ½ each in dimensions, in black ink or paint, and on the upper and most conspicuous part of the cask or package.

§ 2. Any person, company or corporation who shall sell or offer to sell such mixed or adulterated sugars, syrups, honey or molasses containing glucose, grape sugar, or any articles of adulteration, shall expose or sell the same in or from the original packages in which it was consigned from the manufacturer or mixer to the same, and shall be plainly and conspicuously marked or labeled as required in the first section of this act.

§ 3. Any person who shall violate the provisions of this act shall be deemed guilty of a misdemeanor and on conviction thereof shall be liable to a fine of not less than $10 nor more than $200, or to imprisonment in the county jail for not more than 60 days, or both fine and imprisonment in the discretion of the court.

§ 4. This act shall take effect on the first day of June, 1881.

Circulars and Catalogues.—The following Circulars and Catalogues are on our desk:

E. A. Thomas, Coleraine, Mass.—4 pages—Choice Italian Queens and Bees.

Kennicutt & Keyser, Tecumseh, Mich.—4 pages—Poultry and Bees.

Bright Bros., Mazeppa, Minn.—20 pages—Apiarian Supplies.

S. Valentine, Double Pipe Creek. Md.—4 pages—Italian, Albino and Holy Land Queens and Bees.

L. C. Root & Bro. Mohawk, N. Y.—12 pages-Bee-Keeping Supplies, Quinby's New Bee-Keeping, &c.

I. R. Good, Nappanee, Ind.—1 page—Holy Land Bees and Queens.

H. Barber, Adrian, Mich.—1 page—Russell Hives, Italian Queens and Bees.

Geo. H. Lamb, Wilmington, N. C.—1 page—Italian Queens.

J. M. Brooks & Bro., Columbus, Ind.—2 pages—American-bred Italian Queens and Bees, and Apiarian Supplies.

F.A. Snell, Milledgeville, Ill.—18 pages—Bee Hives, Italian Bees and Apiarian Supplies.

H. A. Burch & Co., South Haven, Mich.—40 pages—Bees, Queens and Bee-keepers' Supplies.

Riegel & Drum, Adelphi, O.—8 pages—Italian Bees and Queens and Apiarian Supplies.

A. T. Blauvelt & Co., Blauveltville. N. Y.—16 pages—
Fruit and Ornamental Trees.

Vennor's Predictions for April.

So remarkable have his predictions been fulfilled in the past that we hope we shall not be disappointed in his predictions for May weather during at least a part of this month. The following are his probabilities for April:

> There will be sharp frost in the beginning of April, with a snowfall on the 4th or 5th, but the spring will open favorably, and everything will be pretty well advanced by April 15. Floods may be expected in Chicago about the first week in April, with high winds also prevailing in the early part of the month. Snow-falls are probable about April 5. Navigation is likely to open on Lake Ontario about April 7.
>
> The St. Lawrence will be open about the 9th or 11th, and the first steamship will probably arrive about the 17th or 18th. The weather will be very stormy in the Lower Provinces about the 20th, with very high water prevailing, but in the West, April will be a dry month. There will be warm weather just following the 20th, ending in thunderstorms on the 24th and 25th. Snowstorms are probable in the far West on the 25th and 26th, and snow-falls are not unlikely to occur in England at the close of the month. The month will end wet and cold, but, on the whole, will be like a May month.

Two Queens in a Hive.—Mr. Fradenburg says: "I think I can throw a new ray of light on this subject, which is now-a-days attracting some attention among bee-keepers. I have come to the conclusion that there are but just two causes or conditions in which two laying queens will be found in a hive at once—the first is the superseding of an old and failing queen, in which case each queen seems to have a sort of reverence for the other; the second condition is that the bees in one part of the hive do not know at all times what is going on in another part of the hive. This assertion may raise a storm of opposition among the fraternity, but I believe I have the positive evidence to support it."

☞ We have received a very nice specimen of thin foundation for surplus boxes, made on the Root Mill, from G. W. Stanley, Wyoming, N. Y.

☞ This issue of the BEE JOURNAL, the first in the month, goes to all the subscribers of the Weekly, Monthly and Semi-Monthly. Should any of the latter wish to change to the Weekly, they can do so at any time, by paying the difference.

☞ We can supply but a few more of the back numbers to new subscribers. If any want them, they must be sent for soon.

☞ California has had its floods, and now the Northwest is having a severe experience in the same line. According to Vennor our turn is next. Let all be watchful, and prepare in time, if possible, to avoid loss.

☞ Single copies of the JOURNAL are sent postage paid for 5 cents each.

☞ Constitutions and By-Laws for local Associations $2 per 100. The name of the Association printed in the blanks for 50 cents extra.

☞ The Volume of the BEE JOURNAL for 1880, bound in stiff paper covers, will be sent by mail, for $1.50.

☞ When changing a postoffice address, mention the *old* address as well as the new one.

SELECTIONS FROM OUR LETTER BOX

Correction.—In the BEE JOURNAL for March 16, page 85, the number of my colonies is given as 25; it should be 85. So far as I can learn they are in good condition. I winter them in the cellar. I have been handling bees for 6 years. Osage is a growing city, and will consume all the honey produced in this locality. There are about 500 colonies of bees in Mitchell County, and I will do my share in supplying the market with honey.

CHAS. FOLLETT.

Osage, Iowa, March 21, 1881.

Good Enough.—My bees wintered well. I only lost one out of 92 colonies. Some have lost all they had; others 2/3, etc. The spring is backward. As yet we have had but few days that bees could fly.

W. H. HOWLETT.

Union, Ky., March 22, 1881.

Using Old Combs.—Is it not dangerous to use combs with dead brood in from defunct colonies? Is there not danger of getting foul brood started? I have a good many of them, and I am undecided whether to melt them up or save them. The losses here have been fearful. I do not think there are 10 live colonies in Dixon outside of my apiary, and I have lost ⅓. Those lost were packed in dry chaff, as Prof. Cook's Manual directs, in Langstroth and Simplicity hives, while Root's chaff hive has come out ahead, only 2 or 3 hives of this kind have failed, out of about 30 chaff hives in use. There were as many as 10 or 12 different apiaries in and near Dixon, and I can count 8 of them now that are all dead; the most of them were small, containing from 6 to 30 colonies each. And the end is not yet. Those yet alive may die soon unless spring opens at once.

B. F. PRATT.

Dixon, Ill., March 27, 1881.

[It is hardly possible there is a great deal of dead brood in the combs to be removed. We should not hesitate, if the brood is dry and shrunken, to place the combs in strong colonies; but if the brood is putrid and ropy, and sticks to the cells, we would not wish to use them, as it is easy to imagine the possibility of foul brood or other diseases arising therefrom. If, as we suspect, your combs are filled with starved bees, you can easily remove them by adopting the plan recommended in the Weekly BEE JOURNAL of March 16, page 86. Mr. H. T. Collins gives his method in this number of the JOURNAL.—ED.]

Never Give Up.—Bees are nearly all dead. A long winter is the cause, of course. "Never give up" is and must be our motto, but we must learn not to venture too far without experience to back us.

N. J. LONGSDON.

Byron, Ill., March 26, 1881.

Good Prospect.—There is every prospect of a prosperous season now, as we are having rain enough, and I never saw bees in better condition. I commenced on the 3d of March to divide colonies, rear queens, &c. I have my hives nearly completed for the season's operations. There is quite a contrast between northern Iowa and southern Cal. for bee-keeping. I commenced the last season with 48 colonies in very poor condition, and this season I start with 108 in extra good condition; in fact, the poorest colony I have is in as good condition as the best was last season at the same time.

ELISHA GALLUP.

Santa Paula, Cal., March 18, 1881.

Spring Come at Last.—The weather is spring-like here, and has been since March came in. The snow has all disappeared, and our roads are dry and dusty. As I write the blue birds and robins are singing merrily.

HENRY ALLEY.

Wenham, Mass., March 23, 1881.

Come Gentle Spring.—I have 60 colonies in the cellar; they are in poor condition and will all die if Vennor does not give us fine weather soon, so that the bees can have a flight. They were all right March 1st. I like the Weekly much better than the Monthly.

WM. C. GRAY.

Pre-emption, Ill., March 24, 1881.

Bees All Right.—I have lost 2 colonies out of 16, and the remaining 14 are strong. I had them packed in buckwheat chaff, which is considered the best packing we can get. I have wintered for 4 years with it, and had success. In the winter of 1877 and 1878 I had 45 colonies packed in kiln-dried shavings and wheat chaff: but 4 were packed in buckwheat chaff and those 4 lived; the rest died. There was a very heavy loss around here among those that were left unpacked. I am well pleased with the Weekly BEE JOURNAL.

W. S. BAIR.

Rollersville, O., March 24, 1881.

Lost 6 out of 100 Colonies.—The snow is all gone now and our bees have had several flights. On the 16th they gathered some pollen; but this has been the most disastrous winter among bees in Maryland for many years; 75 per cent of all the bees in north Md. are dead. We had a very poor honey season last year, except 5 weeks during the first crop of red clover, which ended about the 1st of July; and after that but little honey was gathered. The bulk of the loss was from neglect or starvation. As I had a fair demand for queens and I was breeding for improvement I kept up the queen breeding until the last of Oct., and my bees were in poor condition for an ordinary winter; much more for such a one as we have just passed through. I have lost 6 colonies at home, that starved; I have 96 left in fair condition. I wintered in a cellar expressly arranged for the purpose; it is perfectly dark, and the temperature in this place was kept all through the winter at 46° and 47°. All those that wintered in cellars fared the best. I am much pleased with the Weekly. I should lose a friend were I to be deprived of it. I wish it every success.

S. VALENTINE.

Double Pipe Creek, Md., March 22.

Vexed and Perplexed.—When I go into my bee lot and look around I am vexed over the situation and perplexed to know what to do with my hives and combs. I put into winter quarters 16 colonies (all blacks) and now have one, very weak. I have a lot of nice, well-made and painted hives on hand, and a lot of combs. As I have never handled Italian bees, and have concluded to purchase, and I hear they are larger than the blacks, will you please answer these 2 questions in the BEE JOURNAL: Are comb cells of the black bee too small for the Italians to raise brood in? Will it not cramp them in size? Will it be safe to feed the thin uncapped honey that has caused dysentery to other bees? The bees in this vicinity are all dead. Success to the BEE JOURNAL.

D. S. KALLY.

Mansfield, Ind.

[The difference in size of cells is not perceptible. If bees are flying freely, you can feed the thin honey with impunity.—ED.

Ventilation.—I have met 14 different persons in the last few days that had, last Nov., 168 colonies of bees altogether; now they have in the aggregate 57 living; these were mostly in frame hives, on the summer stands, and left to care for themselves. Nearly all died with plenty of honey to have carried them through. This, I think, will be about the average loss in the counties of Champaign, Piatt and Moultrie, in this State. Wm. H. Beckwith started in the winter with 18 colonies in Langstroth and box hives, with plenty of bees and honey in each hive. The hives were very poorly made, being open at the corners, with a board laid on top to keep the rain or snow from falling directly into the hive. Nearly all of them set on blocks from one to two inches from the bottom board; they were ventilated better than any bees I have seen this season; he has 16 colonies to day, alive, and apparently in good condition. Perhaps there is more in ventilation than chaff hives or cellars. Will some one please rise and explain?

S. GOODRICH.

Urbana, Ill., March 23, 1881.

Bees Confined 5 Months.—Yesterday my colonies of bees had their first flight since the last week in Oct., having been confined to their hives 5 months, lacking 2 or 3 days only. This is a month longer than I have ever had them confined to the hive without a flight, during the past 12 years, and to my very great satisfaction as well as astonishment, I do not find a single dead colony. Some 5 or 10 are considerably diseased, and a few are almost sure to be found queenless. I expect to lose from 5 to 15 between this and honey harvest. Bees generally have wintered very poorly in this section. From ½ to 2/3 of all the bees put in winter quarters last fall, have died. I winter entirely in chaff hives, and from what I hear I judge that that method of wintering has succeeded better than any other during this past winter.

O. O. POPPLETON.

Williamstown, Iowa, March 25,1881.

Orchard Apiary.—The following is my report for 1880; My bees came through very strong in spring, and bred rapidly, and were in excellent condition to take advantage of fruit bloom, which lasted about a week, during which time they filled the hives well with honey, and it is well that they did, for raspberry and white clover proved a total failure here, on account of bad weather in June. My surplus all came from basswood, which produced well for about 10 days. Notwithstanding the poor season, and it was the poorest we we have had, I realized a profit of over $8 per colony; but went into winter quarters strong and with plenty of good wholesome stores.

E. A. THOMAS.

Coleraine, Mass., Feb. 1, 1881.

Loss in Cellars, etc.—I put 95 colonies in the cellar on Nov. 15. I took them out yesterday, which was the first day they could fly with safety since about the first of last Nov. Loss 4 (one probably queenless when put in, and 3 starved). A few are weak, but most of them are in good condition. This has been a very hard winter on bees that were not properly cared for. Those left out are nearly all dead, as far as heard from. A good many have died in cellars and special repositories, for want of a knowledge of the proper conditions for success. I like the JOURNAL very much.

J. E. HUNTER.

Wyoming, Iowa, March 25, 1881.

Blasted Hopes.—For the first time, I enroll myself in the army of "blasted hopes." My 150 colonies of bees are (all but one) among the things that were. I had no honey from them last season, or at least none but what I fed back in the fall, and a good many were entirely destitute, so that I broke them up. Some had a little honey and I gave that to those that had a little more, and still had 150 left. Winter set in early, about the middle of Nov., before I had packed any of them. I waited for milder weather so that I could pack them, but that did not come until the 6th of March. Never a day did my bees have a fly until then; and then I had but one colony fly, and I hoped they would come through all right in my double hives, but they did not. Most of them had plenty of honey. All of those having honey had brood and some of them young bees; such had soiled the combs. The one that is alive is strong and has plenty of brood. I thought that bees did not commence to raise brood until a warm spell, but it seems I was mistaken. I have heretofore boxed up a part and left a part unprotected, and have had success with both. I think I should have done better to have boxed them up this year. I have now a lot of empty hives and a great plenty of nice combs. I shall not need any foundation nor bee supplies this year; but need bees to cover my combs. In the BEE JOURNAL for March 9 Mr. Doolittle's article on "Bee Moths" contains an error. A year or two ago I was at a friend's in Allegan Co., in this State, in September, and he told me that the moths were killing all of his bees. I then thought like Mr. D., that they did not hurt good colonies. He said they did and showed me swarms, with new white combs, the queen and brood all right, but the sides of the hives were white with moth cocoons. They were all black bees; I do not think they would have troubled Italians. I like the WEEKLY BEE JOURNAL very much, but do not know that it will be of much value to me now. The cause of the death of my bees was, I think, the long steady cold, with no flight; and not the extreme cold; but why did one of them live through all right? It was just like the rest in the fall.

A. C. BALCH.

Kalamazoo, Mich., March 12, 1881.

The Outlook Encouraging.—The loss in wintering has been very heavy in this county during the past cold winter. In one apiary near me, in Langstroth hives, only 5 are now alive out of 100 last Oct. My home apiary of 175 colonies last Oct., mostly in closed-end Quinby-frame hives, wintered on summer stands packed with fine straw and chaff, now numbers only 115. The loss has been much the heaviest in open end frames, especially so in metal corner frames. Out of 78 in such frame hives only 2 colonies are left. Last year was the poorest season I have had in 12 years; I had but one natural swarm during the season. White clover was a failure; there is but little basswood near here. By feeding I kept my bees in good condition for the fall harvest; smart weed furnished a very little; Spanish needle (the best honey plant in this section) was a total failure; this is the 2d year in 12 that it has failed. I had one apiary near the Illinois river which contained colonies last spring, in Quinby hives. The early part of the season was poor, but I had during the season 21 natural swarms and over 3000 lbs. of section honey for sale, with a surplus of 3000 lbs. in brood frames; more than enough to winter them, which I brought to my home apiary. The above harvest was wholly from smart weed, which was grown on overflow land near the Mississippi and Illinois rivers. The loss in this apiary will not exceed 10 from all causes. All are strong and booming. The soft maples are now in bloom; every fair day the bees are carrying in pollen and a very little honey; the elm will soon be in bloom furnishing an abundance of pollen for rapid queen rearing. With favorable weather I expect a spring harvest from the willow privet bush and red haw; the honey from these is very light colored and of excellent quality. Your hopeful outlook for the coming season is very cheering. The Weekly is both a pleasure and a necessity with me.

A. T. WILLIAMS.

St. Charles, Mo., March 24, 1881.

Severe Winter, but Bees All Right.—This has been the most severe winter experienced by the oldest inhabitant in Ky. I have 14 colonies well packed in chaff, on their summer stands; 3 in the star chaff hive, 9 in the simplicity with tight bottom and portico, and 2 in the simplicity hive. Banked each of them on 3 sides with snow; 12 faced south, 2 north, with no winter passages; used the enameled cloth contrary to friend Muth's advice. I packed on each side of those in single-wall hives with loose chaff, also on the top. I had from 3 to 7 frames in each hive. All wintered equally well, and to-day the queens are doing their duty nobly, shut in on from 2 to 3 frames, and crowded with bees. I think the chaff hive unnecessary for this climate, but it is necessary to pack them well with an absorbent in order to bring them safely through our generally changeable winters. Success to the Weekly; it is growing in interest from week to week, and its coming is anxiously longed for.

C. H. DEAN.

Mortonsville, Ky., March 18, 1881.

Winter Bee House.—My bees have wintered splendidly in my winter bee house.

L. CARSON.

Frederick, O., March 24, 1881.

Bees Wintered Well.—Bees on the summer stands without protection have wintered poorly in this vicinity. I have fifty colonies in Quinby hives, packed in oat chaff and cut straw, that have all wintered well so far. Most of the bees in this vicinity are in box hives, and nearly ½ of them are dead as far as heard from.

E. DEUEL.

Portlandville, N. Y., March 24, 1881.

Bees in fair Condition.—My bees are in a fair condition, on the summer stands. I put into winter quarters 66 colonies; lost 3 and bought 14, making 75 in fair condition. Owing to old age and poor health I intend to sell my bees, although I regret it very much. Last year was a very poor one for honey. I obtained about 600 lbs. of comb honey, which I sold for 15 cts. a lb., and I had one swarm. I like the Weekly BEE JOURNAL very much. I had one colony of bees swarm out on the 15th of this month; they flew around about half an hour and then went back into the hive again. I examined them on the 17th and found the colony strong, with combs all dry and nice, and about 25 lbs. of honey, some pollen, with eggs and brood in all stages. They are now satisfied.

J. J. QUINN.

Corydon, Ky., March 25, 1881.

The Survival of the Fittest.—Another blizzard struck us yesterday; the weather is not so cold, but the high winds and heavy fall of snow make it more disagreeable than any day of the cold zero weather. Bees will get another set-back by their brood chilling. Those that come out in good condition this spring can be considered tough citizens, and no mistake.

JOS. M. BROOKS.

Columbus, Ind., March 30, 1881.

Half of the Bees Dead.—There is a loss of more than one-half of the bees in this county. I am well pleased with the Weekly BEE JOURNAL.

W. A. HERRON.

Indianola, Iowa, March 28, 1881.

Wintered Without Loss.—I believe I am the only one in this county that has not lost more or less bees this winter. My bees were all transferred from box hives last fall, their stores taken away, and they were fed on syrup. They have wintered without any loss of bees. I have bought of Mr. Muth, of Cincinnati, some extracted basswood honey, and shall dilute it with sugar syrup and feed this spring. My bees all have more or less brood now.

W. T. CLARY.

Clarysville, Ky., March 29, 1881.

Wintered Safely.—Bees are dying very rapidly in this section of country. I have 18 colonies; 2 are weak, but I have lost none so far. I bought a Cyprian queen from a firm in the East. She wintered all right, but her workers are hybrid Italians. I lost one last fall by foul brood. I am much pleased with the Weekly BEE JOURNAL.

WM. H. GARIHAN.

Northumberland, Pa., March 28, 1881.

Chaff Did Not Save the Bees.—The bees in this vicinity are mostly dead. Chaff did not save them from the effects of the past severe winter.

L. HUBBARD.

Waldron, Mich., March 25, 1881.

Wintered in Chaff.—Three-fourths of the bees in this neighborhood are dead. I packed mine with chaff on the summer stands, and they came out nice and strong. I am a beginner, and derive much benefit from the BEE JOURNAL, which is a welcome visitor.

EVAN B. HADLEY.

Deming, Ind., March 29, 1881.

Eleven Swarms from One Colony.—I commenced the last spring with 13 Italian and 4 black colonies, and in the fall I had 70; lost 6 in wintering by being queenless. I have sold 4, and now have 60 doing well. I had 11 swarms from one colony and its increase, besides 50 lbs. of honey. The BEE JOURNAL is *the* bee paper, and I wish it success.

E. CARR.

Leesville, Texas, March 14, 1881.

A Visit Every Week, Very Pleasant.—My bees have been at work on the soft maple for the past week. I commenced the winter with 31 colonies; I now have 21; many of them are very strong; some died with plenty of honey in their hives. Last season was a poor one, giving no surplus. I think there will be a heavy loss of bees here. I thought I would not like the Weekly BEE JOURNAL as well as the monthly, but I would not exchange it now for any monthly, because I can hear from my bee-keeping friends every week. I wish it great success.

N. DAVIS.

Emporia, Kan., March 28, 1881.

Buds are Swelling; Spring is Coming.—By the JOURNAL I notice that the winter has been a disastrous one to bees. It must be hard to report a loss of ½ or ¾; and some of the reports even say—"all dead." I am afraid that some of the bee-keepers in this section can say ditto to these reports. The loss around here is greater than there is any need of, on account of the carelessness of farmers in preparing their bees for winter; some of them leave them out on the summer stands without any protection whatever, and of course the result is plain. I have wintered mine in the cellar for the past 2 seasons without any loss, except one that starved this winter; and I am to blame for that in not knowing their condition when I put them in the cellar. I think that now all fear of loss is past, for my bees are doing as well as could be desired. They are breeding considerably, and are all bright and healthy. The snow is going off slowly, at last, and we may look for spring soon. The maple trees are full of swelling buds—it is too early to say anything about fruit bloom; I don't know whether it is killed or not. White clover looks well where the snow is off, and it promises well for the coming season.

HARRY G. BURNET.

Blairstown, Iowa, March 26, 1881.

Bees About All Dead.—I put my bees into winter quarters in the Mitchell hive, packed with clover chaff at each end of the hive about 6 inches thick, and over the top with cushions with the same, about 4 inches thick, all on the summer stands. My loss is now about 2 per cent. The snow is now from 12 to 15 inches deep; this does not look very encouraging; the bees in this part of the country are about all dead. I like the JOURNAL much better as a Weekly than before?; it gives us *fresh* news.

S. M. OLDHAM.

Reynoldsburg, O., March 30, 1881.

Double-Walled Hives.—A large proportion of bees have died in this vicinity this winter. I have lost 6 colonies out of 16. I am using Hill's double-walled winter bee hive. I lost none wintered in these hives, but every one in Langstroth hives died. I wintered on summer stands and one hive had as much protection as another. I feel sure I should have saved all if I had used the double-walled hive; those that died had honey enough in the hive to have wintered them through, if they could have got at it. My bees are carrying pollen every day they can be out.

J. R. WILCOX.

Utica, Ind., March 29, 1881.

Losses in Wintering.—Having seen no report from this vicinity, I have taken some pains to ascertain the extent of the losses of the bee-men of this part of Wayne county, Ind. I have reports (some of them indirectly) from 34. Ten report a total loss; 8, 90 per cent.; 6, 80 per cent.; the others from 33 to 25 per cent. The average loss of colonies will probably be 80 per cent., and those colonies which survive are very much reduced in numbers. Most of them were left unprotected on the summer stands. I find that those that were taken into the cellar before the severe cold of November, came through with small loss, while those taken in after ice had accumulated in the hive, fared the worst of all. I am an advocate of cellar wintering, having never lost a colony until the present winter, and that is through neglect in not taking them in early; I lost 3 this time. I am convinced that dysentery (the one great cause of our loss) could have been much mitigated by keeping an even temperature, which cannot be done out-of-doors, and had we removed their unsealed, poor food and fed them candy instead, our reports would have been different. Two colonies thus treated by me came through in good condition. My bees gathered pollen and honey yesterday from the willow. Maple will be in bloom in a few days.

M. H. WOLFER.

Richmond, Ind., March 28, 1881.

Local Convention Directory.

1881. *Time and Place of Meeting.*

April 2—S. W. Iowa, at Corning, Iowa.

5—Central Kentucky, at Winchester, Ky.

Wm. Williamson, Sec., Lexington, Ky.

7—Union Association, at Eminence, Ky.

E. Drane, Sec. pro tem., Eminence, Ky.

7—N. W. Ohio, at Delta. Ohio.

13—N. W. Missouri, at St. Joseph, Mo.

D. G. Parker, Pres., St. Joseph, Mo.

May 4—Tuscarawas and Muskingum Valley, at Cambridge, Guernsey Co., O.

J. A. Bucklew, Sec., Clarks, O.

5—Central Michigan, at Lansing, Mich.

10—Cortland Union, at Cortland, N. Y.

C. M. Bean, Sec., McGrawville, N. Y.

11—S. W. Wisconsin, at Darlington, Wis.

N. E. France, Sec., Platteville, Wis.

12, 13—Texas Bee-Keepers' Association, at McKinney, Collin Co., Texas.

W. R. Howard, Sec., Kingston, Hunt Co., Tex.

Sept. — —National, at Lexington, Ky.

—Kentucky State, at Louisville, Ky.

Oct. 18—Ky. State, in Exposition B'd'g, Louisville, Ky.

W. Williamson, Sec., Lexington, Ky.

☞ In order to have this Table complete, Secretaries are requested to forward full particulars of time and place of future meetings.—ED.

CLUBBING LIST

We supply the Weekly **American Bee Journal** and any of the following periodicals, for 1881, at the prices quoted in the last column of figures. The first column gives the regular price of both:

	Publishers' Price.	*Club.*
The Weekly Bee Journal (T. G. Newman)		$2 00
and Gleanings in Bee-Culture (A. I. Root)	3 00	2 75
Bee-Keepers' Magazine (A. J. King)	3 00	2 60
Bee-Keepers' Exchange (J. H. Nellis)	2 75	2 50
The 4 above-named papers	4 75	3 75
Bee-Keepers' Instructor (W. Thomas)	2 50	2 35
Bee-Keepers' Guide (A. G. Hill)	2 50	2 35
The 6 above-named papers	5 75	5 00
Prof. Cook's Manual (bound in cloth)	3 25	3 00
Bee-Culture (T. G. Newman)	2 40	2 25

For Semi-monthly Bee Journal, $1.00 less.

For Monthly Bee Journal, $1.50 less.

Honey and Beeswax Market
BUYERS' QUOTATIONS.

CHICAGO.

HONEY—The market is plentifully supplied with honey, and sales are slow at weak, easy prices. Quotable at 18@20c. for strictly choice white comb in 1 and 2 lb. boxes; at 14@16c. for fair to good in large packages, and at 10@12c. for common dark-colored and broken lots. Extracted, 8@10c.

BEESWAX.—Choice yellow, 20@23c.; dark, 15@17.

NEW YORK.

HONEY.—Best white comb honey, small neat packages, 14@16c.; fair do., 14@16c.; dark do., 11@12; large boxes sell for about 2c. under above. White extracted, 9@10c.; dark, 7@8c.; southern strained, 80@85c.

BEESWAX.—Prime quality, 20@23c.

CINCINNATI.

HONEY.—The market for extracted clover honey is good, at 8@10c. Comb honey is of slow sale at 16c. for the best.

BEESWAX.—18@22c.

C. F. MUTH.

SAN FRANCISCO.

HONEY.—The "Vigilant" takes 600 cases to Liverpool. There is a slightly improved feeling consequent upon a little more inquiry, but prices show no material appreciation. Discouraging reports are received from the southern part of the State, as to the prospects of the coming crop, but other sections give promise of an abundant yield. With a good supply yet on the market, prices are not apt to be buoyant until the anticipated failure is more fully settled. We quote white comb, 12@13c.; dark to good, 9@11c. Extracted, choice to extra white, 5½@6½c.; dark and candied, 5@5½c.

BEESWAX.—22@22½c., as to color.

STEARNS & SMITH, 423 Front Street.

San Francisco, Cal., March 11, 1881.

A Smooth Complexion can be had by every lady who will use Parker's Ginger Tonic. For promptly regulating the liver and kidneys and purifying the blood there is nothing like it, and this is the reason why it so quickly removes pimples and gives a rosy bloom to the cheek. See notice.

☞ We have prepared Ribbon Badges for bee-keepers, on which are printed a large bee in gold. Price 10 cents each, or $8.00 per hundred.

☞ Notices and advertisements intended for the Weekly BEE JOURNAL must reach this office by Friday of the week previous.

☞ Instead of sending silver money in letters, procure 1, 2 or 3 cent stamps. We can use them, and it is safer to send such than silver.

☞ The Michigan Bee-Keepers' Association will convene in Pioneer Rooms of the State Capitol at Lansing, May 5. The following is the programme:

Regular order of business.

Annual address by Pres. W. J. Ashworth.

Address by T. G. Newman, editor of American Bee Journal; subject, Rise, Progress, Present Condition and Future Prospects of American Apiculture.

Essay—Profitable extent of bee-keeping, by James Heddon, Dowagiac.

Essay—Requisites of an Apiary, by H. A. Burch, South Haven.

Essay—Some important facts in bee-keeping, by Prof. A. J. Cook, Michigan Agricultural College.

Discussions and remarks.

Examination of exhibits.

All exhibitors of supplies are requested to send samples to the Secretary, with prices and descriptions attached, and all transportation charges must be prepaid by the exhibitors.

GEO. L. PERRY, *Sec.*

☞ Programme of the Northwestern Bee-Keepers' Union, to be held at Hastings, Minn., May 17, 1881:

1.—Address of Welcome, by J. N. Searls.

2.—Reports of committees.

3.—Reports from all—number, kind and condition of bees.

4.—A paper by Pres. A. Tidball, on honey-producing plants and flowers.

5.—A paper by Dr. P. Barton, of St. Paul, on honey as food and medicine.

6.—Apiary culture and our fairs, by Hon. William Avery, of St. Croix Falls, Wis.

7.—A paper on sales of honey, by F. B. Dorothy, of Taylor's Falls, Minn.

8.—A paper on wintering bees, by L. Day, of Farmington.

9.—Progressive bee-culture, by J. G. Teter.

The above subjects will be open for discussion. In addition to the above, the following subjects are suggested:

1.—Essential properties of a good bee hive.

2.—How to prevent and cure foul brood.

3.—How to prevent spring dwindling.

4.—Comb Foundation, with dividing and natural swarming.

Appointment of committees.

Election of officers. Adjournment.

☞ All bee-keepers are cordially invited. Entertainment free.

F. B. DOROTHY, *Sec.*

☞ The Northern Indiana Bee-keepers Association will hold their regular meeting at the Court House, at Valparaiso, Ind., April 7th, 1881, at 2 o'clock p. m., for the election of officers, and for the transaction of any other business that may come before the meeting.

J. B. DECROW, *Sec.*

☞ The North Western Wisconsin Bee-keepers Association will meet at Germania Hall, La Crosse, Wis., on Tuesday, May 10, at 10 a. m. All interested in bee-keeping are requested to be present.

L. H. PAMMEL, JR., *Sec.*

☞ The Semi-Annual meeting of the Champlain Valley Bee-Keepers' Association will be held at Bristol, Addison Co., Vt., May 19, 1881.

T. BROOKINS, *Sec.*

☞ The next meeting of the N. W. Illinois and S. W. Wisconsin Bee-Keepers' Association, will be held at H. W. Lee's, 2 miles n.w. of Pecatonica, Winnebago county, Ills., on the 17th of May, 1881.

J. STEWART, *Sec.*

☞ On account of unfavorable weather the convention at Monroe Centre, Ill., met on Feb. 8, and there being but few present, adjourned to the same place on March 29, 1881.

A. RICE, *Pres.*

☞ The Texas Bee-Keepers' Association will hold their third annual Convention at Judge W. H. Andrews' apiary, in McKinney, Collin Co., Texas, on the 12th and 13th days of May, 1881.

WM. R. HOWARD, *Sec.*,
Kingston, Hunt Co., Texas.

☞ Sample copies of the Weekly BEE JOURNAL will be sent *free* to any names that may be sent in. Any one intending to get up a club can have sample copies sent to the persons they desire to interview, by sending the names to this office.

☞ It would save us much trouble, if all would be particular to give their P.O. address and name, when writing to this office. We have several letters (some inclosing money) that have no name. Many others having no Post-office, County or State. Also, if you live near one postoffice and get your mail at another, be sure to give the address we have on our list.

HEADQUARTERS IN THE SOUTH,
for the Manufacture and Sale of
BEE-KEEPERS' SUPPLIES
SIMPLICITY
AND
LANGSTROTH HIVES
AND FRAMES
The New All-in-one-piece Sections!

Having purchased, from A. I. Root, a machine for making these sections, I am ready to supply them in any quantity. Comb Foundation, made of pure yellow wax, and worked on shares; Honey and Wax Extractors, Knives, Bee Smokers, etc.

Italian Queens & Bees!

all bred from imported mothers of my own importation. Dollar Queens, ready April 1st, $1.10, until June 1st; after, $1.

Tested Queens from 1st March to 1st November. Safe arrival guaranteed and all queens sent by mail. I send no queens that I would not have for myself. Full colonies of Italian Bees from $5 to $8.50, according to quantity, etc. Early 4-frame nucleus, with Tested Queen, $5. No black bees in the neighborhood. Send for my Illustrated Catalogue of prices, etc. Address,

PAUL L. VIALLON, Bayou Goula, La.

The Sweet Home RASPBERRY

Is the largest, most productive, (bearing bushels per acre,) firmest, best shipping Raspberry ever introduced; perfectly hardy, been tested by 36° below zero; sells the best; costs less to pick, because it is firmer; and uniformly larger than any other Black Cap. For Circular address,

9m2t

D. D. PALMER, New Boston, Ill.

Friends, **if you are in any way interested in**
BEES OR HONEY
We will with pleasure send you a sample copy of our
Monthly Gleanings in Bee-Culture,

with a descriptive price-list of the latest improvements in **Hives, Honey Extractors, Artificial Comb, Section Honey Boxes**, all books and journals, and everything pertaining to Bee Culture. *Nothing Patented.* Simply send your address on a postal card, *written plainly,* to A. I. ROOT, Medina, O.

A NEW PLAN.—For one dollar we will send full printed directions how to prevent the end of the sheet of wax from adhering to the rolls in making comb foundation. Address,

1m6t

SMITH & SMITH, Kenton, Ohio.

ITALIAN QUEENS.

Tested Queens	$1 50
Warranted Queens	1 00
Cyprian Queens, untested	1 00

As most all the Dollar Queens I sold last year were pure, I will warrant them this year.

J. T. WILSON,

Mortonsville, Woodford Co., Ky.

1m6t

Italian, Cyprian & Holy Land Queens,

Single Queen, Tested	**$2 00**
Single Queen, Untested, laying	**1 00**

By mail, safe arrival guaranteed.

8-frame colony	**$6 00**
3-frame nucleus	**3 00**
2-frame nucleus	**2 50**

By express, safe arrival guaranteed.

W. P. HENDERSON, Murfreesboro, Tenn.

1m6t

15 One-Cent Stamps

Will pay for our exhaustive pamphlet on raising, handling and marketing extracted honey.

COLONIES
WITH
Imported Cyprian and Italian Queens,
Of our own Importation,
GUARANTEED PURE AND GENUINE.

Our **Comb Foundation** was awarded the diploma at the North-Eastern Bee-Keepers' Convention held in February.

Smokers, Knives, Extractors, &c.

Price List, with 3 samples of Comb Foundation, free.

CHAS. DADANT & SON,
Hamilton, Hancock Co., Ill.

9smtf

FLAT-BOTTOM COMB FOUNDATION,

high side-walls, 4 to 16 square feet to the pound. Circular and samples free

J. VAN DEUSEN & SONS,
Sole Manufacturers,
Sprout Brook, Mont. Co., N. Y.

11tf

C. Olm's Comb Foundation Machine.

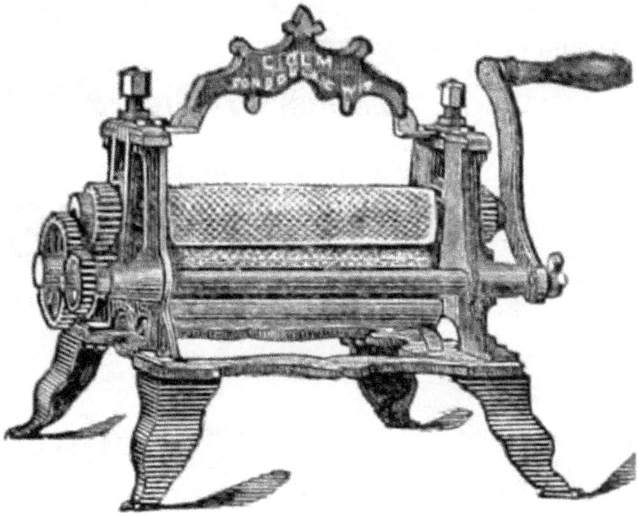

9-inch.—Price $25.00.

The cut represents the 9-inch machine; the cheapest made until now. Send for Circular and Sample.

C. OLM, Fond du Lac, Wis.

JOHN BAXTER, Pickering, Ont., agent for Canada.

1mtf

SECTIONS AND HIVES.

We will make the Dovetailed or the "Boss" One-Piece Section any size up to 5×6, for $5.00 per 1,000. Material for Langstroth hive, 50c., including brood frames.

JAMES FORNCROOK & CO.

Watertown, Jeff. Co., Wis., March 1, 1880.

Take Notice.—There is a patent pending on the "Boss" one-piece Section. 9mtf

JOSEPH D. ENAS,

(Sunny Side Apiary,)

Pure Italian Queens, Bees, Colonies

Nuclei, Comb Foundation, etc.

Address. **Napa, Napa County, Cal.**

9m6t

ITALIAN QUEENS.

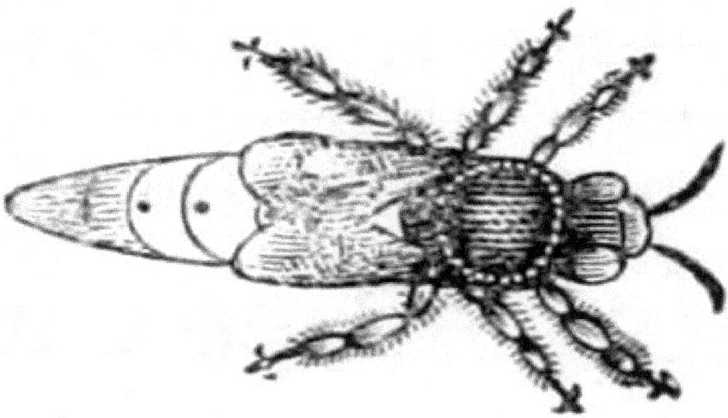

1881. 1881.

Safe Arrival Guaranteed!

I am prepared to furnish queens of the purest grade, all bred from Imported Stock:

Untested Queens, in May and June	$1 50
Untested Queens, in July and after	1 00
Tested Queens, in May and June	2 50
Tested Queens, in July and after	2 00

I guarantee all my Queens to be purely mated.

☞ Send for price list—free.

L. C. McFATRIDGE, M. D.,
Carroll, Carroll Co., Ind.

9m6t

SUPPLIES FOR THE APIARY,
FOR 1881.

It is to every person's interest, when they wish to purchase anything, to go where they can get the most for their money. State on a postal card just what you want, and we will let you know by return mail what we will furnish it for. No Circulars. Address,

HIRAM ROOP, Carson City, Mich.

12mtf

FRANCES DUNHAM,
Inventor and Sole Manufacturer of the
DUNHAM
FOUNDATION
MACHINE,

AND DUNHAM
COMB FOUNDATION,

☞ New Circular and Samples free. ☜

FRANCES DUNHAM,
DEPERE, BROWN CO., WIS.

1sm6m

TWENTY-EIGHTH YEAR.

65 First Premiums, Medals and Diplomas.—Send postal card, with name and address, for my new Illustrated Circular and Price-List, containing valuable information to all bee-keepers. CHAS. H. LAKE, successor to the late Richard Colvin, 96 West Pratt Street, Baltimore, Md.

4wtf

MUTH'S
HONEY EXTRACTOR
AND UNCAPPING KNIFE.

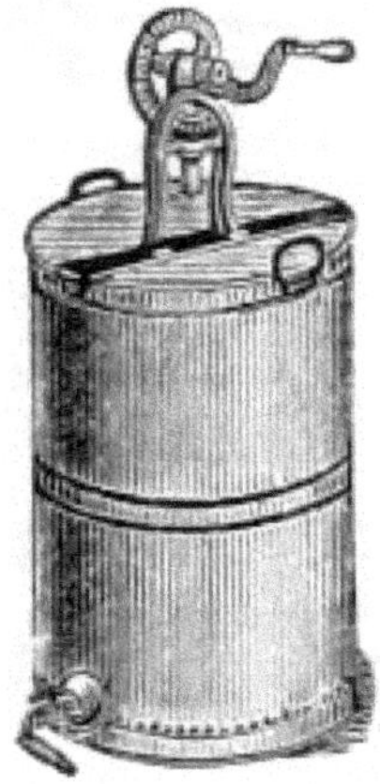

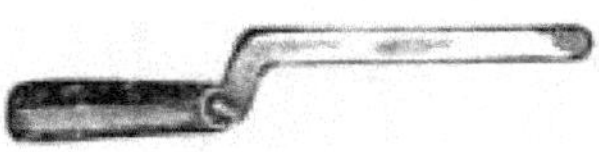

The Extractor is made of all metal, is always ready for use, easily cleaned, and will last a lifetime. In fact, it has only to be used to be appreciated. Every Bee-Keeper should send for my circular giving details about the care of bees and how to get the most Honey.

CHAS. F. MUTH, No. 976
Central Av., Cincinnati, O.

1m1y

WESTERN BEE-KEEPERS can save money by sending for our new Illustrated Circular and Price List of **Apiarian Supplies, Note and Letter Heads, Cards, &c.**

BRIGHT BROTHERS,
Mazeppa, Wabasha Co., Minn.

9m2tp

Books for Bee-Keepers.

Cook's Manual of the Apiary.—Entirely rewritten, greatly enlarged and elegantly illustrated, and is fully up with the times on every conceivable subject that interests the apiarist. It is not only instructive, but intensely interesting and thoroughly practical. The book is a masterly production, and one that no bee-keeper, however limited his means, can afford to do without. Cloth, **$1.25**; paper covers, **$1.00**, postpaid. Per dozen, by express, cloth, $12.; paper, $9.50.

Quinby's New Bee-Keeping, by L. C. Root.—The author has treated the subject of bee-keeping in a manner that cannot fail to interest all. Its style is plain and forcible, making all its readers sensible of the fact that the author is really the master of the subject. Price, **$1.50.**

Novice's A B C of Bee-Culture, by A. I. Root.—This embraces "everything pertaining to the care of the honey-bee," and is valuable to beginners and those more advanced. Cloth, **$1.25**; paper, **$1.00.**

King's Bee-Keepers' Text-Book, by A. J. King.—This edition is revised and brought down to the present time. Cloth, **$1.00**; paper, **75c.**

Langstroth on the Hive and Honey Bee.—This is a standard scientific work. Price, **$2.00.**

Blessed Bees, by John Allen.—A romance of bee-keeping, full of practical information and contagious enthusiasm. Cloth, **$1.00.**

Bee-Culture; or Successful Management of the Apiary, by Thomas G. Newman.—This pamphlet embraces the following subjects: The Location of the Apiary—Honey Plants—Queen Rearing—Feeding—Swarming—Dividing—Transferring—Italianizing—Introducing Queens—Extracting—Quieting and Handling Bees—The Newest Method of Preparing Honey for Market, etc. It is published in **English** and **German**. Price for either edition, **40 cents**, postpaid, or $3.00 per dozen.

Food Adulteration; What we eat and should not eat. This book should be in every family, where it ought to create a sentiment against the adulteration of food products, and demand a law to protect consumers against the many health-destroying adulterations offered as food. 200 pages. Paper, **50c.**

The Dzierzon Theory;—presents the fundamental principles of bee-culture, and furnishes a condensed statement of the facts and arguments by which they are demonstrated. Price, **15 cents.**

Honey, as Food and Medicine, by Thomas G. Newman.—This is a pamphlet of 24 pages, discoursing upon the Ancient History of Bees and Honey; the nature, quality, sources, and preparation of Honey for the Market; Honey as an article of food, giving recipes for making Honey Cakes, Cookies, Puddings, Foam, Wines, &c.; and Honey as Medicine, followed by many useful Recipes. It is intended for consumers, and should be scattered by thousands all over the country, and thus assist in creating a demand for honey. Published in **English** and **German**. Price for either edition, **6c.**; per dozen, **50c.**

Wintering Bees.—This pamphlet contains all the Prize Essays on this important subject, that were read before the Centennial Bee-Keepers' Association. The Prize—$25 in gold—was awarded to Prof. Cook's Essay, which is given in full. Price, **10c.**

The Hive I Use.—Being a description of the hive used by G. M. Doolittle. Price, **5c.**

Extracted Honey; Harvesting, Handling and Marketing.—A 24-page pamphlet, by Ch. & C. P. Dadant, Hamilton, Ill. This gives in detail the methods and management adopted in their apiary. It contains many good and useful hints, and is well worth the price—**15c.**

Practical Hints to Bee-Keepers, by Chas. F. Muth, Cincinnati, Ohio; 32 pages. This pamphlet gives Mr. Muth's views on the management of bees, and embraces several of his essays given at Conventions, etc. It will be read with interest by beginners as well as those more advanced in the science of bee-culture. Price, **10c.**

Kendall's Horse Book.—No book can be more useful to horse owners. It has 35 engravings, illustrating positions of sick horses, and treats all diseases in a plain and comprehensive manner. It has a large number of good recipes, a table of doses, and much other valuable horse information. Paper, **25c.**

Chicken Cholera, by A. J. Hill.—A treatise on its cause, symptoms and cure. Price, **25c.**

Moore's Universal Assistant contains information on every conceivable subject, as well as receipts for almost everything that could be desired. We doubt if any one could be induced to do without it, after having spent a few hours in looking it through. It contains 480 pages, and 500 engravings. Cloth, **$2.50.**

Ropp's Easy Calculator.—These are handy tables for all kinds of merchandise and interest. It is really a lightning calculator, nicely bound, with slate and pocket for papers. In cloth, **$1.00**; Morocco, **$1.50**. Cheap edition, without slate, **50c.**

☞ Sent by mail on receipt of price, by

THOMAS G. NEWMAN,
974 West Madison Street, **Chicago, Ill.**

EMERSON BINDERS.

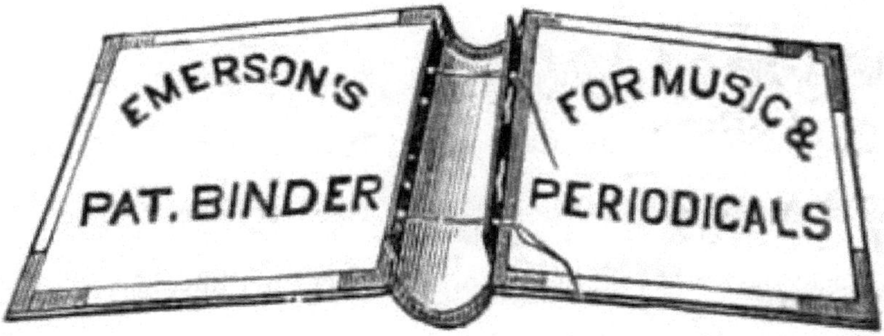

EMERSON'S PAT. BINDER FOR MUSIC & PERIODICALS

☞ **Binders for the Weekly Bee Journal, of 1881**, cloth and paper, **postpaid, 85 cents.**

We can furnish Emerson's Binders, gilt lettered on the back, for AMERICAN BEE JOURNAL for **1880**, at the following prices, postage paid:

Cloth and paper, each 50c.

Leather and cloth 75c.

☞ We can also furnish the Binder for any Paper or Magazine desired.

THOMAS G. NEWMAN,
974 West Madison Street, **Chicago, Ill.**

RATES FOR ADVERTISING.

A line will contain about **eight words**; fourteen lines will occupy one inch of space.

One to three weeks, each insertion,	**20** cts. per line.
Four weeks or more, each insertion,	**18** cts. per line.
Eight weeks or more, each insertion,	**15** cts. per line.
Thirteen weeks or more, each insertion,	**12** cts. per line.
Twenty-six weeks or more, each insertion,	**10** cts. per line.
Fifty-two weeks or more, each insertion,	**8** cts. per line.

Special Notices, 50 cents per line.

Advertisements withdrawn before the expiration of the contract, will be charged the full rate for the time the advertisement *is* inserted.

Transient Advertisements payable in advance.—Yearly Contracts payable quarterly, in advance.

THE AMERICAN BEE JOURNAL is the oldest Bee Paper in America, and has a large circulation in every State, Territory and Province, among farmers, mechanics, professional and business men, and is, therefore the best advertising medium for reliable dealers. Cases of *real* imposition will be exposed.

THOMAS G. NEWMAN,
974 West Madison Street, **Chicago, Ill.**

Bees for Sale.

I wish to sell my **75 Colonies of Bees**, all in movable frame hives. In fair condition. I will take **$4.00** per Colony.

J. J. QUINN,
Corydon, Henderson Co., Ky.

14w1t

QUEENS
& BEES.

Tested, $2; Untested, $1; Black Bees, $6; Italians, $10; Plymouth Rock Eggs, $1.25 per dz., and the best and cheapest Hives made. Circular free.

[14w1tp] H. BARBER, Adrian, Mich.

Hives, Sections,
AND BOXES.

Material for Langstroth Hives, including brood frames, 40c. each; Lewis' V-shaped groove one-piece Sections, any size to 6×6, $5 per 1,000; Lewis' one-piece Honey Boxes of all sizes, $2 to $4 per 100, including glass; Dovetailed Sections, any size to 6×6, $4 per 1,000. Manufacturing experience of 20 years.

Send for Price List.

G. B. LEWIS,
Successor to Lewis & Parks, Watertown, Wis.

N.B.—There is no patent on the Lewis One-Piece Section.

12mtf

ITALIANS AND HYBRIDS—30 or 40 Colonies for sale low. Queens and Nuclei after May 15th. Address,

R. M. ARGO,
Lowell, Garrard County, Ky.

12w3t

WANTED—You to send for our Circular and Price list of **American-Italians**. Address,

JOS. M. BROOKS & BRO.,
Columbus, Ind.

12w6m

MAMMOTH RUSSIAN SUNFLOWER SEED—Excellent for poultry, and yields an abundance of fall honey. Flowers from 10 to 20 inches in diameter. Price **25c.** per pkg., postpaid.

L. M. WAINWRIGHT, Noblesville. Ind.

14w1tp

PRIZE COMB FOUNDATION, 10 sq. ft. per lb., with natural base. Send for samples.

G. W. STANLEY, Wyoming, N. Y.

14-1tp

THE BRITISH BEE JOURNAL, AND BEE-KEEPER'S ADVISER.

The *British Bee Journal* is published monthly at $1.75, and contains the best practical information for the time being, showing what to do, and when and how to do it. **C. N. ABBOTT**, Bee Master,

School of Apiculture, Fairlawn, Southall, London.

WORTH WILL WIN.

Truly, "Time sifts the wheat from the chaff." We lead in Smokers. Our Double-blast Smoker is perfection. See what "the most extensive bee-keeper in America" says of our Quinby Smoker:

Cherry Valley, N. Y., March 22, 1881.

After testing your smokers with others of the best make, I do not hesitate to order two dozen for use in our apiaries. When we use a Smoker we make a business of it, running it all day and burning hard maple wood, which tests the construction most thoroughly. Those we have been using admit coals into the bellows, which burn the leather. The tube in your Quinby Smoker running further into the firebox, must prevent this in a great measure.

CAPT. J. E. HETHERINGTON.

If you desire to see a description of the goods we used in securing over 15,000 lbs. of honey from 176 colonies of bees the past poor season, send for our New Illustrated Circular for 1881, which is just ready.

L. C. ROOT & BRO.,
Mohawk, N. Y.

14m1t

Rev. A. SALISBURY,
Camargo, Douglas County, Ill.

Warranted Italian Queens, $1.00; Tested Italian Queens, $2.00; Cyprian Queens, $2.00; Tested Cyprian Queens, $4.00; 1 frame Nucleus, Italians, $4.00; 1 frame Nucleus, Cyprians, $5.00; Colony of Italians, 8 frames, $8.00; Colony of Cyprians, 8 frames, $10.00. Wax worked 10c. per lb. Pure Comb Foundation, on Dunham Machine, 25 lbs. or over, 35c. per lb. ☞ Send for Circular.

1w1y

DON'T BUY SUPPLIES

Till you have read my new price list for the spring trade. Wax is cheaper now, so I can sell you a fine article of Comb Foundation cheap, and made on the best machine. Italian and Cyprian Queens, Bees, Hives, Sections, etc. Price List free to all.

J. V. CALDWELL,
Cambridge, Henry Co., Ill.

12w6m

Given's Foundation Press.

The latest improvement in Foundation. Our thin and common Foundation is not surpassed. The only invention to make Foundation in the wired frame. All Presses warranted to give satisfaction. Send for Catalogue and Samples.

D. S. GIVEN, Hoopeston, Ill.

1w1y

WILBOR'S COMPOUND OF
PURE COD LIVER
OIL AND LIME.

To One and All.—Are you suffering from a Cough, Cold, Asthma, Bronchitis, or any of the various pulmonary troubles that so often end in Consumption? If so, use "*Wilbor's Pure Cod-Liver Oil and Lime*," a safe and sure remedy. This is no quack preparation, but is regularly prescribed by the medical faculty. Manufactured only by A. B. WILBOR, Chemist, Boston. Sold by all druggists.

QUEENS, BEES, ETC.
IF YOU WISH THE
Best, Gentlest and Most Beautiful Bees,
I am prepared to furnish early Queens.

PURE ALBINO, ITALIAN AND HOLY LAND QUEENS,

Bred from Imported and Select Stock. Warranted to be pure, and safe arrival guaranteed. Also Hives, Novice's Extractor, and Apiarian Supplies generally. Send for Price List. Address,

S. VALENTINE,
Double Pipe Creek, Carroll Co., Md.

14m3t

---

13 EGGS from fine Plymouth Rock or W. Leghorn fowls for $2, or 26 for $3. Will exchange eggs for Queens or Bees.

J. H. THORNBURG,
Winchester, Randolph Co., Ind.

14w3t

I HAVE NOW OVER 300 COLONIES

of Pure Italian Bees, in good condition, in 10 frame Langstroth hives. Orders for

ITALIAN QUEENS,
Nuclei and Full Colonies,

are now being booked and will be filled in rotation as received, commencing about June 1st., at the following prices:

Tested Queens, each	$2.50
Tested Queens, per half-dozen	13.50
1 frame Nucleus, with Tested Queen	5.00
2 frame Nucleus, with Tested Queen	5.50
3 frame Nucleus, with Tested Queen	6.00
4 frame Nucleus, with Tested Queen	6.50
Full Colonies, each	12.00
Full Colonies, in lots of 5, each	10.00
Full Colonies, in lots of 10, each	9.00

I will use all possible care in preparing the above for shipment, but cannot guarantee safe arrival, except on queens any distance less than 1,000 miles.

ALSO
100 COLONIES
OF
BLACK AND HYBRID BEES,

In Langstroth hives, in quantities of not less than 5 colonies at **$8.00** each, which I will ship direct from the South, at any time after April 15th.

Also, 200 Colonies of Native Bees,

in Box Hives, delivered on Mississippi River Steamboat any time after April 15th, in lots of 10 or more, at **$6.00** each.

☞ The Colonies of Hybrids and Natives are very strong in bees reared this spring, and combs well filled with brood. They can be transferred or divided by May 1st, and increased in time for white clover and basswood surplus.

ALFRED H. NEWMAN,

972 West Madison St., Chicago, Ill.

THE ORIGINAL

Patented Jan. 9, 1878, and May, 1879; Re-issued July 9, 1878.

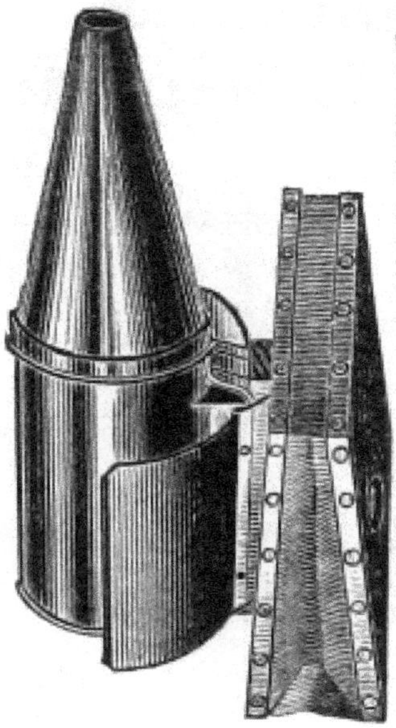

If you buy a Bingham Smoker, or a Bingham & Hetherington Honey Knife you are sure of the best and cheapest, and not liable to prosecution for their use and sale. The largest bee-keepers use them exclusively. Twenty thousand in use—not one ever returned, or letter of complaint received. Our original patent Smokers and Honey Knives were the only ones on exhibition at the last National Bee-Keepers' Convention, 1880. Time sifts the wheat from the chaff. Pretensions are short-lived.

The Large and Extra Standard have extra wide shields to prevent burning the fingers and bellows. A real improvement.

Send postal card for testimonials.

Bingham &, Hetherington Honey Knife	2	in.,	$1 00
Large Bingham Smoker	2½	"	1 50
Extra Standard Bingham Smoker	2	"	1 25
Plain Standard Bingham Smoker	2	"	1 00

Little Wonder Bingham Smoker	1¾	"	75

If to be sent by mail, or singly by express, add 25c. each, to prepay postage or express charges.

To sell again, apply for dozen or half-dozen rates.

Address,

BINGHAM & HETHERINGTON,
ABRONIA, MICH.

9wtf

EVERY BEE-KEEPER

Wanting anything in the line of Apiarian Supplies should send for my Descriptive Circular. Sent free. Address,

F. A. SNELL,
Milledgeville, Carroll Co., Ill.

13w4t

ITALIAN QUEENS, Full Colonies, Nuclei and Bee Hives specialties. Our **new** Illustrated Catalogue of Bees, Supplies, Fine Poultry, Small Fruits, &c., **Free.** ☞ Send for it and save money.

J. T. SCOTT & BRO., Crawfish Springs, Ga. 2w32tx

R. A. BURNETT.
Successor to Conner, Burnett & Co.,
165 South Water Street, Chicago, Ill.,

GENERAL PRODUCE COMMISSION.
HONEY A SPECIALTY.

We ask you to correspond with us before disposing of your HONEY CROP, as we can be of much service, having constant intelligence from all parts of the country. We would refer to JAMES HEDDON, Dowagiac, Mich., and J. OATMAN & SONS, Dundee, Ill.

1w1y

GOOD WORK
AT FAIR PRICES

HALLOCK & CHANDLER
WOOD ENGRAVERS
& Electrotypers
167 DEARBORN ST.
CHICAGO

1w1y

Florida Land—640 Acres.

☛ CHEAP FOR CASH. ☚

DESCRIPTION.—Sec. 4, township 7, south range west, Franklin county, Florida, situated about 50 miles south of the Georgia line, 25 miles west of the city of Tallahassee, the capital of the State, and about 25 miles northeast of the city of Apalachicola, a seaport on the Gulf of Mexico, and within 2 sections (5 and 6) of the Apalachicola river; the soil is a rich, sandy loam, covered with timber.

It was conveyed on Dec. 31st, 1875, by Col. Alexander McDonald, who owned 6 sections, including the above, to J. M. Murphy, for $3,200, and on Sept. 5th, 1877, by him conveyed to the undersigned for $3,000. The title is perfect, and it is unincumbered, as shown by an abstract from the Records of the county, duly attested by the County Clerk; the taxes are all paid and the receipts are in my possession.

I will sell the above at a bargain for cash, or trade for a small farm, or other desirable property. An offer for it is respectfully solicited. Address,

THOMAS G. NEWMAN,
974 West Madison Street, CHICAGO, ILL.

PARKER'S GINGER TONIC

Ginger, Buchu, Mandrake, Stillingia and many other of the best medicines known are combined so skillfully in PARKER'S GINGER TONIC as to make it the **greatest Blood Purifier** and the **Best Health and Strength Restorer ever used.**

It cures **Dyspepsia, Rheumatism, Neuralgia, Sleeplessness**, and all diseases of the **Stomach, Bowels, Lungs, Liver, Kidneys, Urinary Organs** and all **Female Complaints.**

If you are wasting away with Consumption or any disease, use the TONIC to-day. No matter what your symptoms may be, it will surely help you.

Remember! This TONIC cures drunkenness, is the **Best Family Medicine** ever made, entirely different from Bitters, Ginger

Preparations and other Tonics, and combines the best curative properties of all. Buy a 50c. bottle of your druggist. None genuine without our signature on outside wrapper.

HISCOX & CO., Chemists, New York.

PARKER'S HAIR BALSAM The best and most economical Hair Dressing

CPSIA information can be obtained
at www.ICGtesting.com
Printed in the USA
LVHW011240061021
699678LV00001B/77

9 789355 118875